Love 21

Emma Russell

BookLeaf Publishing

India | USA | UK

Presentation by *BookLeaf Publishing*

Web: www.bookleafpub.com

E-mail: info@bookleafpub.com

ISBN: 9789360949020

First edition 2024

Adam my inspiration and light of my life

ACKNOWLEDGEMENT

Thank you to my family who inspire me daily and adam my soulmate who keeps me sane.

The last two poems in this book are especially close too my heart light of my life was written to Adam in his Christmas card and Jessica's poem was written when my niece passed away at a week old.

Sweetest love

I love you deep with all my heart,
And when I sleep my feelings start,
They drift into a wonderland,
Each time I hold your soft, sweet hand,
My fears drift away like falling sand.

I know your love is like a dove,
All full up with soft, sweet love,
And when I think of you and smile,
I sit about and think awhile,
My heart still full of harsh denial.

In my heart I need to know,
Do you want to stay or go,
I know it's hard to answer straight,
But I can no longer wait,
Please don't say its much to late.

In the darkness of the night,
You always bring me into the light,
You still always drive me wild,
With your love so soft and mild,
As gentle as a tiny child.

My promise

I promise to bring you happiness,
And then to bring you love,
I promise to bring you the heavens,
And then the stars above.

I promise to give you everything,
That a lover ever could,
I promise to give you pleasure,
Like you never thought I would.

I promise to leave you everything,
My heart,body and soul,
I promise to leave you my laughter,
As soft as a tiny doll.

I promise to be here always,
You fill my heart with pride,
This love will last forever,
One day I'll be your bride.

Feelings of life

Darkness is a wonder a mystery untold,
A soft and subtle pleasure never bright or bold,
A careless tender whisper of secrets new and
old,
Spirits cold and evil like the soul you once sold.

Sunlight is a gift from the stars above,
A glimmer of happiness a telltale sign of love,
A sweet and sacred messenger high up like a
dove,
A mystery of power that holds u like a glove.

Love is a passion that comes from the soul,
An everlasting feeling a complete one time goal,
A touch of tenderness that warms like hot coal,
A soft warm feeling like hugging a doll.

Hate is a terror that smothers the heart,
A feeling of loneliness that burns from the start,
A cold sensation that hits like a dart,
A silent corrupter in great works of art.

Soulmates

I feel your pride you feel my joy,
our hearts are joined as one,
Each time we kiss are souls will merge,
Now they are joined as one.

I feel your pleasure you feel my my passion,
Our bodies are joined as one,
Each time we caress are spirits will mix,
Now they are joined as one.

I feel your love you feel my pain,
Our minds are joined as one,
Each time we talk our voices fuse,
Now they are joined as one.

I feel your heart your body and soul,
Our lives are joined as one,
Each time we die we are reborn,
Into this world as one.

Emotions

My spirit awakens whenever you're near,
Then seeps away like a tiny wet tear,
It rolls down my cheek and on to the floor,
As soon as you turn to walk out the door.

My love for you burns like fire,
Hot and rampant with desire,
It flickers when you leave my sight,
But always ends up shining bright.

My smile is true when I see your face,
I'm golden and glowing all over the place,
It grows and it grows as your body gets nearer,
My feelings for you could never be clearer.

The look

I see the look of hunger,
Upon your dampened lips,
A body strong and younger,
Your gorgeous sexy hips.

I see the look of love,
Upon your soft sweet face,
A gift from stars above,
Your warm and kind embrace.

I see the look of pride,
Upon your tender smile,
A feeling deep inside,
Your true and honest style.

I see the look of pain,
Upon you're cheating heart,
A passion so insane,
Your love was false from the start.

I see the look of sadness,
Upon you're tired eyes,
A moment of intense madness,
Your lover slowly dies.

Lovers

You come to me now silent and strong,
With you in my arms I can never go wrong,
I hold you close, I hold you tight,
When you're around it feels so right.

You open your arms and welcome me in,
My love for you burns deep within,
I place my lips upon your face,
Our bodies move with perfect grace.

You whisper to me the sweetest things,
Our love shines bright like diamond rings,
I kiss your body from head to toe,
And then our passion starts to grow.

You run your fingers down my spine,
Oh how I wish you could always be mine,
You leave the bed and walk away,
It's over now and you can't stay.

True love

In your arms my soul is home,
My heart will never be alone,
As long as you are by my side,
My love for you can never hide.

I need your heart I need your mind,
Don't ever leave my soul behind,
I see your smile in the stars,
Our passion locked behind cold bars.

You are my friend you are my lover,
For me there can be no other,
We are one we are strong,
With you in my world I can't go wrong.

Your eyes are soft so true and blue,
I could love no one else but you,
Our love is bigger than the sky,
It will last forever even when we die.

Sweet caress

The sweetest smile is all I see,
Each time you stand in front of me,
Your sexy eyes so clear and true,
I can't help but fall for you.

When you are near I can't be sad,
With you I'm always happy and glad,
In your arms I am content,
My heart does ache with such torment.

I know your heart takes time to heal,
But with my love your heart can feel,
The sweet sensation of happiness,
Each time we touch with tenderness.

You are the sun that lights my life,
With you there is no worry or strife,
You helped me heal now I will help you,
I'll show you love so deep and true.

Moments in time

One moment in time is all it takes,
For a lonely heart to crumble and break,
Shattered pieces on the floor,
Blown away through an open door.

Two moments in time is all you need,
For a haunted soul to open snd bleed,
Dripping liquid crimson red,
Splattered stains across the bed.

Three moments in time is all we had,
For a love so pure to turn dark and bad,
Lonely moments turned it sour,
As the minutes passed the hour.

Four moments in time is all they gave,
For me and you to try and save,
That special bond that made us strong,
Our knowledge of passion that's never wrong.

Life's flame

Caught in the fire that is life,
I hold you close my darling wife,
I whisper words so soft and true,
My burning passion I have for you.

Like kindred spirit's in the flame,
The love in you I'll never tame,
Your soft sweet smile and delicate touch,
I hunger for you oh so much.

We kiss and caress with such desire,
Our love burns stronger than a fire,
The flame is hot and so are we,
So hold me close and let it be.

Our time is up the end is near,
Sweet old age is Upon us dear,
We had a life so strong and full,
So let's not fight deaths hardest pull.

Goodbye my cherub just close your eyes,
We have no other earthly ties,
Born as two and die as one,
I was the moon and you the sun.

Kiss me honey

Kiss me honey in my dreams,
Show me darling sensual things,
Love me baby when you are free,
Virtual passion endless needs.

Seduce me lover end my tears,
Drive me wild under starlight skies,
Comfort my heart endless times,
Lightning strikes in my soul.

Caress me darling aline at last,
Real temptation everlasting pleasure,
Send me wild with desire,
Shadows hide our eternal light.

Sweet desire

Hot, sticky oh so sweet,
You to me are such a treat,
Super, candy can't compare,
To your secret suggestive stare.

Lick your lips and look my way,
I live for this moment every day,
Chocolate, cream my heads a whirl,
My temptress bakery shop girl.

Sprinkles, icing what will I do,
I need to be so close to you,
Smooth, tasty you are to me,
When will you notice I'll wait and see.

Friends

When you kiss me on the cheek,
My heart speeds up and skips a beat,
My body tingles from head to toe,
And lights My soul with a loving glow.

I'd wait eternity for you to see,
You can be happy if your with me,
For now we ate just loyal friends
So let's wait and see how the story ends.

I hope its happy, fun and long,
My feelings for you will always go on,
So these words my love I write to you,
Now to your heart you must be true.

Shattered

Shattered glass on the floor,
You come storming through the door,
Mixed emotions swirl around,
So you throw me to the ground.

Hiding in there room that night,
Children crying what a sight,
Cold and hungry in there beds,
All the hurtful things you said.

Pack your bags get out the door,
I won't take this anymore,
Loves not supposed to be like this,
I need hugs and tenderness.

Time to heal room to grow,
Protect my kids let my love show,
It's for the best the time is right,
This time, I'm strong enough to fight.

Seasons of love

Spring shadows, morning dew,
Rainbow skies for me and you,
Valentines old and new,
Love is in the air.

Summer sun, bodies baked,
Skimpy clothes and make up caked,
Online dating profiles faked,
Love is in the air.

Autumn leaves on the ground,
Winds howling all around,
Treasured items lost now found,
Love is in the air.

Winter wonders everywhere,
Ice, snow and frosty glare,
A wonderland so raw and rare,
Love is in the air.

Passion

Come to me darling I crave for you,
My body is tingling my bloods boiling too,
Open your arms and hold me so tight,
Kiss me all over this feels so right,
From the top of my head to the tips of my toes,
Willbthis feeling last god only knows,
I tremble beside you sated at last,
My loneliness behind me left in the past,
You are my sunrise and I am your moon,
If this lasts forever it would still end too soon.

Pepples on the sand

Pepples on the sand
Hear the ocean roar
My lovevfor you is grand
I never felt it more

Moonlight in the sky
Stars are twinkling bright
Sweet like apple pie
Our love just feels so right

Fire in the hearth
Blanket on the floor
Love bigger then the earth
Safe behind closed doors

Loves embrace

Glass is fragile so are hearts
Keep them safe and nurture them
Keep them full of love and passion
Sweet soft kissess gentle hugs
Keeps them growing more and more
Make the world a better place
Safe and strong in loves embrace

Jessica's poem

With the angels in the sky,
That is where you now fly,
A shining light that warmed our hearts,
A fighting spirit from the start,
My sweetest Jessica.

Our time with you was very swift,
But you were such a special gift,
A dancing queen for daddy dear
A sleeping beauty when mummy's near,
My sweetest Jessica.

I never got to see your smile,
Mybheart is hurt it's in denial,
I think of you my eyes do cry,
I keep on asking why oh why,
My sweetest Jessica.

Light of my life

In the darkness you are my light,
Your soul shining oh so bright,
You gave me hope and love so true.

You gave me passion and tenderness,
When I'm with you there is no stress,
My heart is bursting with my love for you,
All these feelings are so brand new.

You are my forever, my home, my heart,
I wish we had known it from the start,
With you my soul feels whole and strong,
Our love can never fade or go wrong.